PASCUAL

READING POWER

Women Who Shaped History

Elizabeth Cady Stanton and Susan B. Anthony

Fighting Together for Women's Rights

Joanne Mattern

The Rosen Publishing Group's
PowerKids Press™
New York

Published in 2003 by The Rosen Publishing Group, Inc.
29 East 21st Street, New York, NY 10010

Copyright © 2003 by The Rosen Publishing Group, Inc.

All rights reserved. No part of this book may be reproduced in any form without permission in writing from the publisher, except by a reviewer.

First Edition

Book Design: Erica Clendening

Photo Credits: Cover, p. 13 © Bettmann/Corbis; p. 4 © Mansell/Timepix; pp. 5, 16 © Hulton/Archive/Getty Images; p. 6 courtesy Emma Willard School; pp. 7, 8, 9 courtesy Elizabeth Cady Stanton Trust/Coline Jenkins-Sahlin; p. 10 courtesy of the Susan B. Anthony House, Rochester, NY; p. 11 courtesy of the Canajoharie Library and Art Gallery; p. 14 © New York State Historical Association Library, Cooperstown; pp. 15, 21 Library of Congress, Prints and Photographs Division; p. 17 Ontario County Historical Society; p. 18 collection of the Massillon Museum; p. 19 Erica Clendening; p. 20 © AP/Wide World Photos

Library of Congress Cataloging-in-Publication Data

Mattern, Joanne, 1963-
Elizabeth Cady Stanton and Susan B. Anthony : fighting together for women's rights / Joanne Mattern.
  v. cm. — (Women who shaped history)
Contents: Working together — Elizabeth Cady Stanton — Susan B. Anthony — A perfect team — The right to vote.
ISBN 0-8239-6503-1 (lib. bdg.)
1. Stanton, Elizabeth Cady, 1815-1902—Juvenile literature. 2. Anthony, Susan B. (Susan Brownell), 1820-1906—Juvenile literature. 3. Suffragists—United States—Biography—Juvenile literature. 4. Feminists—United States—Biography—Juvenile literature. 5. Women's rights—United States—History—Juvenile literature. [1. Stanton, Elizabeth Cady, 1815-1902. 2. Anthony, Susan B. (Susan Brownell), 1820-1906. 3. Suffragists. 4. Women—Biography.] I. Title.
HQ1412 .M17 2003
305.42'092'273—dc21

2002002938

Contents

Working Together	4
Elizabeth Cady Stanton	6
Susan B. Anthony	10
A Perfect Team	12
The Right to Vote	20
Glossary	22
Resources	23
Index/Word Count	24
Note	24

Working Together

Today, women can vote, go to college, and become whatever they want to be. Not too long ago, women in America could not do any of these things.

Elizabeth Cady Stanton

Elizabeth Cady Stanton and Susan B. Anthony lived in a time when women were not allowed to do the same things as men. They worked together to fight for women's rights.

Susan B. Anthony

Elizabeth Cady Stanton

Elizabeth Cady was born in Johnstown, New York, on November 12, 1815. Elizabeth Cady wanted to do more than girls were allowed to do. She asked a neighbor to teach her the Greek language, something only boys usually learned. She also went to the best school that there was for girls. She was a very good student and learned a lot.

The school that Elizabeth Cady went to was one of the first places where girls could study the same things as boys.

- Elizabeth Cady worked her entire life to change how girls were treated.

"Oh, my daughter, I wish you were a boy!"

—Elizabeth Cady's father said this to her after his son died. Cady worked hard to prove that being a girl was just as good as being a boy.

In 1840, Elizabeth Cady married Henry Stanton. Together, they fought against slavery. However, many groups that they worked with did not let women join their meetings.

Elizabeth Cady Stanton and her friend Lucretia Mott held a meeting of their own. On July 19 and 20, 1848, the first women's rights convention was held. Three hundred people listened to Stanton speak about women's rights.

Henry Stanton

Elizabeth Cady Stanton is shown here with her daughter, Harriet. The Stantons had seven children.

Susan B. Anthony

Susan Brownell Anthony was born in Adams, Massachusetts, on February 15, 1820.

Susan B. Anthony started teaching school when she was seventeen years old. She taught for more than ten years.

Susan B. Anthony became a teacher. She earned less money than male teachers because she was a woman. Anthony wanted women to be treated equally.

Susan B. Anthony was the principal of the Girls' Department at this school (left) in New York State.

Now You Know

Susan B. Anthony made $2.50 each week. Male teachers made $10 each week.

A Perfect Team

Susan B. Anthony and Elizabeth Cady Stanton met in 1851. They had many of the same ideas. Both of them were against slavery and drinking alcohol. Most of all, they both believed that women should have the same rights as men, including the right to vote.

> "The best protection any woman can have ... is courage."
> —Elizabeth Cady Stanton

After Anthony (left) and Stanton (right) met, they were friends for the rest of their lives.

Anthony traveled around the country speaking to people about women's rights. Stanton wrote the speeches that Anthony gave. Stanton mostly stayed at home to take care of her children.

In 1868, Elizabeth Cady Stanton and Susan B. Anthony started working on a newspaper called *The Revolution.*

> "Men, their rights and nothing more: women, their rights and nothing less."
> —saying written at the top of the first page of *The Revolution*

- Stanton and Anthony wrote about women's rights in *The Revolution.*

In 1860, New York passed a law that gave married women control over the money they earned. Stanton and Anthony worked hard to get this law passed.

In 1869, Stanton and Anthony started the National American Woman Suffrage Association. This group worked to get women the right to vote.

- Women from all over the United States joined the National American Woman Suffrage Association.

In 1872, Susan B. Anthony voted in a presidential election. She was arrested, put on trial, and fined $100. Many newspapers wrote about Anthony's trial. The newspapers said Anthony was being treated unfairly.

Susan B. Anthony's trial took place in this courthouse in New York State.

When Stanton's children were grown, she joined Anthony on her travels around the country. Elizabeth Cady Stanton died on October 26, 1902.

This poster is an ad for one of Elizabeth Cady Stanton's speeches in Ohio.

ELIZABETH CADY STANTON.
Saturday Evening, Feb'y 6, 1875.
LECTURE, "OUR GIRLS."

Susan B. Anthony died four years later on March 13, 1906. The two women had worked together for the causes they believed in for 50 years.

When Susan B. Anthony died, only four states allowed women to vote. They were Wyoming, Colorado, Utah, and Idaho.

The Right to Vote

In 1920, the U.S. government passed a law giving all women in America the right to vote. Today, women and men have the same rights.

The work of Elizabeth Cady Stanton and Susan B. Anthony made many people's lives better.

In 1979, Susan B. Anthony became the first woman pictured on a U.S. coin. It is called the Susan B. Anthony Dollar.

Time Line

November 12, 1815
Elizabeth Cady Stanton is born in Johnstown, New York

July 19–20, 1848
Elizabeth Cady Stanton and Lucretia Mott hold the first U.S. women's rights convention in Seneca Falls, New York

February 15, 1820
Susan Brownell Anthony is born in Adams, Massachusetts

1851 *Stanton and Anthony meet*

On November 2, 1920, women voted in a presidential election for the first time. More than eight million women voted.

"There never will be complete equality until women themselves help to make laws and elect lawmakers."
—Susan B. Anthony

1868 *Stanton and Anthony start working on* The Revolution

October 26, 1902 *Elizabeth Cady Stanton dies*

1920 *Women get the right to vote in the United States*

1872 *Anthony is arrested for voting*

March 13, 1906 *Susan B. Anthony dies*

Glossary

alcohol (**al**-kuh-hawl) a colorless liquid in wine, beer, rum, and whiskey

arrested (uh-**rehst**-uhd) having been put in jail for breaking the law

causes (**kawz**-uhz) ideas or goals that many people care about

college (**kahl**-ihj) a school where people can study after high school

convention (kuhn-**vehn**-shuhn) a large meeting

presidential election (prehz-uh-**dehn**-shuhl ih-**lehk**-shuhn) an event held in the United States every four years to vote for a new president

right (**ryt**) something that a person is allowed to do

slavery (**slay**-vuhr-ee) the practice of owning people and forcing them to do work

suffrage (**suhf**-rihj) the right to vote

trial (**try**-uhl) an argument in court to decide a problem

Resources

Books

Sisters in Strength: American Women Who Made a Difference
by Yona Zeldis McDonough
Henry Holt & Co. (2000)

The Road to Seneca Falls: A Story About Elizabeth Cady Stanton
by Gwenyth Swain
Carolrhoda Books (1996)

Web Sites

Due to the changing nature of Internet links, PowerKids Press has developed an on-line list of Web sites related to the subjects of this book. This site is updated regularly. Please use this link to access the list:

http://www.powerkidslinks.com/wsh/ecsa/

Index

A
alcohol, 12
arrested, 17

C
causes, 19
college, 4
convention, 8, 20

P
presidential election, 17, 21

R
Revolution, The, 14, 21
right, 5, 8, 12, 14, 16, 20–21

S
slavery, 8, 12
suffrage, 16

T
trial, 17

Word Count: 468

Note to Librarians, Teachers, and Parents

If reading is a challenge, Reading Power is a solution! Reading Power is perfect for readers who want high-interest subject matter at an accessible reading level. These fact-filled, photo-illustrated books are designed for readers who want straightforward vocabulary, engaging topics, and a manageable reading experience. With clear picture/text correspondence, leveled Reading Power books put the reader in charge. Now readers have the power to get the information they want and the skills they need in a user-friendly format.